finishing school

michaela coplen

ignitionpress

First published in 2022
by **ignition**press
Oxford Brookes Poetry Centre
Oxford Brookes University
OX3 0BP

Cover design: Flora Hands, Carline Creative

A CIP record for this book is available
from the British Library

ISBN 978-1-9161328-8-7

Contents

If I ever find out just what this word can mean,
I'll be the smartest bird the world has ever seen!

Big Bird, 'Abc-Def-Ghi Song'

Apple

All you have to be is good.
Good is a dog that sits and stays.
So the teacher nods, ascending.
Bad is an apple in the eye.

In school you are so quiet.
You can play the quiet game.
Then the mind begins this squeaking
like a mouse or a garden gate.

Bug

My mother came home with her uniform on and a line where the hat creased her forehead. When she saw that the wall was alive again she went to get the vacuum. I was standing on the table on my toes to get a look: the gap where they came in was like the seeping of a wound. All day I'd watched them trailing in, their quiet congregation. I liked the pattern of their backs. A red that softened everything. Soon she was behind me with the phone against her neck. *No*, she was saying as she plugged the vacuum in, *the less real power that he has the more he'll try to use it.* She handed me the nozzle, went into the other room. I held the sound outside myself and sucked their bodies up.

Chest

Ever so willing a plaything,
when my sister split

the lid off the cedar chest
I would strain to peer

over the edge —
She could see through anything;

paper bags were heavy crowns,
ghosts were also wedding gowns

the bedsheets draped
and grey. She spooled me

in a satin scarf and called me
Salomé; Joan of Arc

and armourless, she leapt
to my defence. In the version

I liked best, she came
too late. She'd lay

my breathless body in the chest,
shut the lid, hurl herself

on top and wail — I would be quiet.
How many unmarked hours,

half-believing, we could lie there —
testing who would break

first, bring me back to life.

Dress

The mind becomes more various
as the girl is hanging clothing —
shirts and dresses damp to touch
all pinned up in a line —

I could be like this or this!
she thinks and they stand to attention —
a tournament of headless dolls
that lunge and tilt and twist —

Egg

Holding to my mother at the lip
of the public bath — *Look*
these men have penises!
I tell her and she laughs

a laugh that skims her shoulders
like the loosing of a robe —

I've learned the hidden body parts,
want them to know I know:
the diagram, the terms
I trace one letter at a time.

In school they warn about
the girl, the unexploded mine
she found alone —
how she dug it up and brought it
into class. The changes,
we are taught, will come on fast
and set us ticking —

My grandmother spells out
a trick to navigate the system:
always spend the night with friends
when your husband's
on a mission (a woman who stays

in the house alone at night
must want what's coming).

That summer at the swimming pool
the air was heavy, humming.

Sex was breaking over us
like the breaking of a shell —
            how that slick missile couldn't miss,
            would always find you home.

Figure

How saints in oil paintings hold
an emblem of their death, the instrument
of passion like an ordinary fact. Agatha holds
her severed breasts. How the arrow meant
          to pierce the side
          is already lodged in the side.

My mother gave up both her breasts
and the hourglass turned over.
Her sutures healed while I grew hips,
broad nipples that twinged to cover —
          tenderly the edges of the flesh
          becoming flesh.

Grasp

There's a basement under everything.
Memory prefers to stay outside, to stand
at the top of the stairs. The girl

goes down without looking. Her hair
pulled into a bun. Dust suspends
in beams of light. Her feet
like a dancer's feet.

You can't be alive and untouchable.

The man who follows after
moves his hand along the railing

and his movement churns the air.

Hair

Afterward, she handles
it like someone handles
hair. First she tries to smooth
it back into the same high knot. When
this begins to come undone she draws
it down like a curtain, spreads the tendrils
out across her ears, around her neck. She gathers
it to one side after she begins to sweat, and
it makes her tilt to balance. She cuts
it sharply back, but the ends stick out
at angles and they fall into her eyes. As
it grows, she tries to work
it into different braids, learns to manage
its consistency, the source that is never not there.

I

Writing lines; confined;
sent away for education —

a girl might well be bad
with such a punishment
her privilege.

Instead, the weight
of early hours. Day
and more of it coming.

The body, newly saddled,
works itself into the ground:
on the paper route; in the ticket box;
at the tables, bent to serve.

Always saving up for something.

On the front of the brochure
a class of girls, poreless,
balance books and apples
on their heads.
The assumption of their laughter
like a key inside the chest:

If I test score; if I scholarship.
If I finish the finishing school.

The mind a twisted
bedsheet rope I
lower to escape —

Jackpot

I am no longer spinning
my wheel — I cannot
buckle down and lucky

I have worked for your
expensive smile —
I dressed me in potential

I repeat: I will not
spin the wheel.
I maintain: I have learned
my lesson.

(If you wink my way again
then I will give it one more go)

Knot

The stretch of concrete off the road
where the new-builds were never built —
where in the dark and his dad's black car
we kept the engine off —
was the place of our necessity

the hush where we would hide ourselves
past highway lights, the railway bridge,
the cows in their low blue barn

and when we parked, with swollen
words, an automatic chuckle
he would eager and unbuckle
I would shift myself to task —
ever-willing subject of the list
I had to tick

and most nights that was it —
a clutch, a minute then of rest,
a fog of breath we'd smear around
the windows with our shirts

but one night, we reversed,
he wanted, yes he really did, he was sure
he could, I said he could, I had no hints
to give — I just watched him

from inside me; I tightened
in the grip: that slip knot
I could never slip (I couldn't
let myself slip).

Letter

You can't climb a ladder while looking back.

Not for the field and its shuttering flowers.
Not for the stream you soothed your ankles in

its water slow and cold. Or the pen
where a swayback mare is pacing, waiting

to be fed. Not for the neighbours' house,
all boarded up, so light comes out in slats.

Not for the quarry growing paler
as the moon comes close,

the walls you filled with expletives
and promises you meant. Not for

the lightning bugs all quivering
in sex-numb glow. Not for the red

where a distance ripens.
The ladder creaks but won't

give way — a step that's only
wide enough for you to sit alone.

And the letter you still haven't opened.

You aren't prepared to know — but from here
this life already looks like the sketch

of a place you've left: how the lines
all progress to their vanishing points,

two roads leading out of town.

Middle

My mother and I are both eighteen —
I'm driving, she's hitching a ride. Her stop's

a couple hours off, it's been a stifling
summer, no she doesn't mind

the windows down, it's fine if I go fast! She holds her
bag between her knees,

leans the seat back; all the fields
are full of passing time, a second crop of hay.

We chat. She has this laugh. We trade
particular opinions (what makes a view

worth stopping for; would you rather be lucky or rich).
We're both leaving home for college. We hold our breath

across the bridge. We talk about each house we pass
like future lives to live. There's really

no good time to tell her. We close
the middle distance, the road

beneath us groaning where the concrete's
wearing thin. The radio

fades out and in
with songs that we both know, and we

go on like that for a long while, both humming,
both facing ahead.

Nest

Midnight after move-out day, the dorm
is open doors. Those of us who stay
to work get started, making claims:

in one room there's a rolled-up rug
with hints of Malbec stain; another boasts
a window fan, new copies of all the books.

I start off with a bedside lamp
and knee-high rubber boots; J rides by
on a wheelie chair, distributes
swigs of gin; someone down the hall
is shouldering a mini-fridge —
then we hear

this child-like shrieking. We stop,
fall into search — growing
urgent, tracking down the sound
behind a final door —

We find a rabbit rattling its cage
on the dorm room floor. It quiets now,
shifts on its wooden chips in trepidation.

We trade some looks amongst ourselves —
V says she'll take it in, and we

resume our private scavenging.
I don a fluffy robe, play
the game where I can build a house
from what they leave behind.

Organ

Alone in a distant city, keeping scrupulous receipts.
I justify my coffee to a board I'll never meet,
grant myself a new indulgence. Loneliness
is an open text, a spigot with a metal grip
that I turn off and on. Like an archive, I'll take
anything. I picnic on the lawn. Every day I use
the language I'm ashamed to have perfected:
how I gesture to a need, knowing the gesture is

enough. At the entrance of a church, I touch
the basin out of habit, render hours
unaccountable — my fingers dripping
blessings. In the sex shop on the corner,
all the toys are on display — in memory they
hang in lines, the pipes of a giant organ.

Prize

Take, for example, Sor Juana: no fear of showing off. Opened up for interview, she holds them all at bay — the way *a royal galleon... might fend off a few canoes.*[1] Sweat pools down her upright back as men draw in around her. *My hair grew fast*, she will later write, *my understanding slow.*[2] In 'First Dream', a soul becomes untethered from its spine. Centuries later, Sylvia Plath considers a graduate scholarship: *Only a million people want them; no competition really.*[3] And Flannery O'Connor writes to God: *I do not mean to be clever although I do mean to be clever on 2nd thought and like to be clever & want to be considered so.*[4] Plath decides she wants the same, prepares an application. The pragmatist, she secures her psychiatrist's recommendation — a *big strip tease* the selection board will [*shove*] *in to see.*[5] In 'Fulbright Scholars', Hughes recalls her hair for what it hid. *Prize*: the purse, the pursed lip. How it means: *to open by force.* The college used to make each woman stand, nude, for the camera — it was said to teach them posture, how to better hold the self.

---

1 Octavio Paz, tr. Margaret Sayers Peden, *Sor Juana, or, the Traps of Faith* (Cambridge, MA: Harvard University Press, 1988), 98.

2 Paraph., Juana Inés de la Cruz, tr. Margaret Sayers Peden, *Poems, Protest, and a Dream: Selected Writings* (New York: Penguin, 1997), 15.

3 Sylvia Plath, 'January 26', *The Unabridged Journals of Sylvia Plath*, ed. Karen V. Kukil (New York: Anchor Books, 2000), no. 164.

4 Flannery O'Connor, *A Prayer Journal*, ed. William A. Sessions (New York: Farrar, Straus & Giroux, 2013), 6.

5 Sylvia Plath, 'Lady Lazarus', *Collected Poems*, ed. Ted Hughes (New York: Harper & Row, 1981), 244-246.

Question

More life than my allotted life
the wind at my ankles, unasked
the mind moving on like light through light
and the spine to ask for more.

More life than my allotted life
the wind at my ankles, unasked
the mind moving on like light through light
and the spine to ask for more.

Rings

It's late in our season of waiting.
The fig tree on the corner grows

heavy, exquisite. For seven months
I've paced the green

circumference of my life. I'm lucky —
there's a humdrum here. A room

with an unworried view. Today
she calls me with the news: they're punching

through the walls. And have I heard
two girls I know from school

have been shot in the head? I'm blanking
on the faces, picture apples (cored)

instead, she tells me one of them was pregnant
with the shooter's child. Meanwhile

the latest candidate, what votes will count
or not — forgive me this

my everyday. All that I
left, forgot. Outside,

the orange god of sun
is taking off his rings.

In school, we learned the fleeing girl
transforms into a tree. Then we learned

the core of every living tree is dead: heartwood,
the hardest wood, which every year surrounds,

as cells surround a neural stem
to form the foetal spine.

Stem

Winter and likewise bitter
in the university garden, I step inside
the glass house where money makes

all things grow. In humid air
the hyacinth congeals
like beaten cream. Lilies
hold their pistils up,
their orange stamens
swaying. From outside the reach
of the cocoa tree, you can't see its
decaying; it's at
the joints of branches
where the fruited body

rots. I won't be adopted so easily.
The automated spraying; the hands
that come to feed the trapping plants
their flies and shit. A vine that supplicates the light
by opening a fist. My father
gave me everything
he could. I need so little.

Cut stems hover
in a glass that's half
water, half air.

Tubes

The hospital waiting room was overfull of arms.
I held a notebook against my knee, its edge

a stretched-out coil — the pen I finished
rested there, an empty plastic tube. Above us

was the buzzing sound of two fluorescent tubes,
a conversation hovering between the light

and noise. Afterward, I padded out
into a tiled tube — the hallway lined with tubes

of talk, a clutch of small disasters. The street
was already dark with rain. Water puddled

into streams and streamed to sunken
tubes — the tubes that hung above

the street were full of power, fatal.
There was nothing to do but walk in it.

The sky was grey, immutable. Window lights
came on, revealing tubes of daily life —

children moving, separately, through parallel
routines. I turned my key inside its tube —

What I fear the most is everything I might
become. A tube moves through me, doggish

pulls around me its ambitions; body
my commodity, my test tube, my tomb.

Urn

The photos you show at the funeral should emphasize my beauty.
There she is in a sweeping dress! Her red car is
speeding off somewhere. The truth
is she could've had her pick; the truth
is she never remembered. True beauty
is expensive. Serve wine, or even better, that
blue-bottle gin we like. All I want is
one good measure, all
the music that the damaged organ manages to chirp. You
should read a poem first — I don't know,
but keep it brief. Put a candlestick on
everything. Say time on earth
is cheap; say I spent it all immodestly and
couldn't keep the rest. Later, misremember all
the stories I like best. They'll be better how you
tell them. Fit a form to hold this grief. By then, I won't need
anything — I won't be here to
need — I'll leave you all I am and want and could and have and know.

View

If I were more like my mother, I'd know what to do
with all these ends — chicken bones, tomato stems,
the inner ribs of peppers. Another thing for the list of things

I'll ignore until I can't: spiderwebs just out of reach,
the puddles beneath the fridge. Honestly, I don't
remember much about her cancer. It happened

in a different room it was happening so fast.
Last night, in a fit of genius, we nailed the doorstop
to the floor. Now I can see almost everything:

the triplets in the garden, the women smoking
on their steps, a collection of silver cans.
The windows of the funeral home on the corner

are papered over — crosswords and the tabloid ads
for local naked ladies. Where I grew up, the major roads
are lined with these invitations. Trucks

shudder to a stop. The pawn shops are always open.
The ghost town only miles away has smouldered
for sixty years — fire caught a vein of coal

and no one can put it out. Here,
I watch the city trains emerge
from underground. We brace against

the frequency — they pass at different speeds.
You're going somewhere, aren't you? The pavement
winks like a lesson, and the mattress they pushed

from the neighbour's house when she died
is still on the kerb — folded, holding its
ankles, flashing the whole wide street.

Walls

Reaching up, against the stretch of wall we've
patched with filler — sanding down
the rough of it — I feel his warm, unhurried hands
unfold against my waist, the way they question
for a place that moves to meet his touch.
To turn to him, as evening sun illuminates
the dust, is to grasp the body as a prism
held, unlacing light. We move ourselves together
through the rush of falling night: our favoured
range of motions, an encouragement of limbs.

As we sleep we brush the dead. The plaster
dimples in. By morning, all the puncture marks
are evident again: the wall, its softened
pockets, proving how much it will take.

X

Reversed, we start in check.

I have always hated chess
(a game you win by not wanting)

but backward, every move
becomes an exercise in love:

my rook appears in his opening
palm; I steady his queen

with a single touch. Pieces
bloom in every square

his bishop leaves behind.
We pause to watch

the pathways turn
inside each other's minds —

the pawns, unknotting,
shuffle home like they

could start again —
but the match goes on

rewinding. We stand,
shake hands,

the arc of our release
like how the tongue

of a stopped bell swings.

Yawn

The time travellers crop up everywhere. Their costumes are very good. They're careful, they've had the briefing. Look away when she starts looking back. There are more in crowded places; there is normally one on the train. They pretend to be kids or creeps if they want leeway for the staring — the tickets they are sold determine how close they can get. At the bar they watch her drinking. At the school they watch her read. All the highest payers look over her shoulder at the screen. (Thanks to convention, they aren't allowed in her most private moments.) She figured it out a while ago. She yawns to check their attention. She watches mouths pop open in response, like baby birds. So as not to disturb the timeline, she keeps doing what she would do.

Zipper

In half-light you tape all the pages to a wall,
the writing cramped, inscrutable; then you
switch on a lamp. Standing there, between
the light and the play of silhouette, this
compulsion to unfasten. You watch
your shape undress, huge and dark across
the lettering. Spellbound, self-possessed
the body advances its argument —

If I uncatch my breath; if I let my hands start
dancing, let them touch me in the dance;
if I point my toes like tiny hooves, the star
of a bad ballet; if I roll my hips to flourish; if I
haven't drawn the shade then who will see me if I
mouth the words, make corresponding sounds?

Notes and acknowledgements

Grateful acknowledgements to the editors of the following publications in which several of these poems first appeared, sometimes in alternate forms: *The Adroit Journal, The London Magazine, The Oxonian Review,* and *The Rialto.* Many thanks to Anne Berkeley for shortlisting 'Egg' and 'View' for the Bedford Poetry Competition, and to Eleanor Perry for awarding 'Rings' the Canterbury Christ Church University Poetry Prize.

This pamphlet is indebted to every poet whose craft has taught me to be crafty, particularly: Donald Justice ('Figure' is after '"There is a gold light in certain old paintings"'); Jack Gilbert ('Hair' is after 'Michiko Dead'); Alicia Ostriker and Emily Dickinson ('Jackpot' is after 'Psalm' and borrows an 'expensive smile' from '"Luck is not chance" (1350)', respectively); Kevin Young ('Letter' is after 'Halter'); Julia Falkner ('Tubes' is after 'Piles'); Terrance Hayes, Gwendolyn Brooks, and John Keats ('Urn' is a Golden Shovel on a line from 'Ode on a Grecian Urn'); and William Carlos Williams ('Zipper' is after 'Dance Russe'). Many thanks are also due to Anne Carson, Marie Howe, Deborah Landau, Ada Limón, Kathryn Maris, and Sharon Olds, whose work is always an education.

The pamphlet's epigraph is taken from *Sesame Street.*

Enormous gratitude to the teachers I've been impossibly lucky to learn from: Matt Fahnestock and Sarah Clayville, who prompted the first inklings; everyone at the Scholastic Art & Writing Awards and the National Student Poets Program, who offered life-changing support; and my professors at Vassar College, particularly Bob Brigham and Paul Kane, who gave me mentorship and room to write when I needed it most.

Profound thanks to the team at **ignition**press, especially to Niall Munro for his uncommon patience and care in editing this pamphlet.

Finally, thanks to my family, friends, Annee, and Sam, for the love and encouragement — for every word, there's another book of words.

MIX
Paper from responsible sources
FSC® C007326
www.fsc.org

Oxford Brookes is committed to the environment.
This document is printed using processes that are:

100% carbon positive
100% EMAS
100% renewable energy
100% ISO14001
100% eco-friendly simitri® toner
100% recycled FSC® stock

Zero % waste to landfill

Printed by **seacourt** – proud to be counted amongst the top environmental printers in the world